The Glory of the Lord

Advent and Christmas Devotionals

Lillie Ammann

Published by:
Lillie's Lovely Little Publishing Company
lillie@lillieammann.com
www.lillieammann.com

Proofreaders:
Alice Goodwin
George Lampe

ISBN: 978-0-9665912-6-2

A Note from the Author

Each year during Advent and Lent, I follow a Bible reading plan for the season. Each day, I journal a short meditation and write a brief prayer. The following year, I have someone proofread my writings and publish them.

This book is being published in 2019 with my personal devotions from 2018. I found the reading plan online; I don't even recall where. It may be the most diverse collections of readings I've used, and I didn't see a strong theme when I was reading them initially. Yet when I read through my meditations this year, I saw a recurring theme: The Glory of the Lord.

Thanks to my friends Alice Goodwin and George Lampe, fellow parishioners at All Saints Anglican Church in San Antonio, for proofreading. I hope you are blessed by these Scriptures, thoughts, and prayers during this holy season.

Profits will be donated to Love for the Least to share the compassion of Christ with an unreached world. L4L shares the Good News of the Gospel with the least and unreached by making disciples of Jesus who make disciples (2 Tim 2:2) and by helping to meet the physical needs of the poorest of the poor. To learn more, visit lovefortheleast.org.

May His blessings abound in your time alone with Him.

Lillie Ammann
November 2019

The First Sunday in Advent

In the beginning was the Word, and the Word was with God, and the Word was God. He was in the beginning with God. All things were made through him, and without him was not any thing made that was made. In him was life, and the life was the light of men. The light shines in the darkness, and the darkness has not overcome it.

There was a man sent from God, whose name was John. He came as a witness, to bear witness about the light, that all might believe through him. He was not the light, but came to bear witness about the light.

The true light, which gives light to everyone, was coming into the world. He was in the world, and the world was made through him, yet the world did not know him. He came to his own, and his own people did not receive him. But to all who did receive him, who believed in his name, he gave the right to become children of God, who were born, not of blood nor of the will of the flesh nor of the will of man, but of God.

And the Word became flesh and dwelt among us, and we have seen his glory, glory as of the only Son from the Father, full of grace and truth. (John bore witness about him, and cried out, "This was he of whom I said, 'He who comes after me ranks before me, because he was before me.'") For from his fullness we have all received, grace upon grace. For the law was given through Moses; grace and truth came through

Jesus Christ. No one has ever seen God; the only God, who is at the Father's side, he has made him known. ~ John 1:1-18

This is one of my favorite Scriptures, beautifully describing the divinity of Jesus Christ. He has always existed, long before He came to earth as a tiny baby to redeem the world. He created everything, and He became man to show us the Father. He came into a world of darkness shining with life and light, yet the world did not recognize Him. Hallelujah! To we who do recognize Him as Lord and Savior, we who believe in Him and give our lives to Him, He gives us grace upon grace and the right to become children of God. As unimaginable as this truth is, it is truth.

Thank You, Lord God, for the unbelievable riches You give to those who love Jesus and do His will. You make us Your beloved children, and You give us abundant life now and forever. Empower me by the Holy Spirit to live my life as a disciple of Jesus Christ, my Lord and Savior, in whose name I pray. Amen.

Monday in the First Week in Advent

Long ago, at many times and in many ways, God spoke to our fathers by the prophets, but in these last days he has spoken to us by his Son, whom he appointed the heir of all things, through whom also he created the world. He is the radiance of the glory of God and the exact imprint of his nature, and he upholds the universe by the word of his power. After making purification for sins, he sat down at the right hand of the Majesty on high, having become as much superior to angels as the name he has inherited is more excellent than theirs.

For to which of the angels did God ever say,
"You are my Son,
   today I have begotten you"?
Or again,
"I will be to him a father,
   and he shall be to me a son"?
And again, when he brings the firstborn into the world, he
says,
"Let all God's angels worship him."
Of the angels he says,
"He makes his angels winds,
   and his ministers a flame of fire."
But of the Son he says,
"Your throne, O God, is forever and ever,
   the scepter of uprightness is the scepter of your kingdom.
You have loved righteousness and hated wickedness;
therefore God, your God, has anointed you
   with the oil of gladness beyond your companions."
And,
"You, Lord, laid the foundation of the earth in the beginning,
   and the heavens are the work of your hands;
they will perish, but you remain;
   they will all wear out like a garment,
like a robe you will roll them up,
   like a garment they will be changed.
But you are the same,
   and your years will have no end."
And to which of the angels has he ever said,
"Sit at my right hand
   until I make your enemies a footstool for your feet"?
Are they not all ministering spirits sent out to serve for the
sake of those who are to inherit salvation? ~ Hebrews 1:1-14

Jesus is divine; He is the Son of God; He is above the angels, who are ministering spirits who serve those who are saved. This entire passage is so powerful, but this sentence may be the most awe-inspiring: "He is the radiance of the glory of God and the exact imprint of his nature, and he upholds the universe by the word of his power." He radiates the glory of God and His nature is exactly the same as that of the Father—there is no question about His deity. Amazingly, there is so much power in His *Word* that He upholds the world ("sustains everything" in other translations) by it.

Lord God, I know that Jesus is Your Son, equal with You as part of the Godhead along with the Holy Spirit. I know He is divine, and I know He is powerful. But I am simply in awe that He sustains everything by His Word. He doesn't have to do anything but speak, and everything holds together. Help me to appreciate how powerful and amazing that is. In the name of Jesus. Amen.

Tuesday in the First Week in Advent

For every high priest chosen from among men is appointed to act on behalf of men in relation to God, to offer gifts and sacrifices for sins. He can deal gently with the ignorant and wayward, since he himself is beset with weakness. Because of this he is obligated to offer sacrifice for his own sins just as he does for those of the people. And no one takes this honor for himself, but only when called by God, just as Aaron was.

So also Christ did not exalt himself to be made a high priest, but was appointed by him who said to him,
"You are my Son,
    today I have begotten you";

as he says also in another place,
"You are a priest forever,
    after the order of Melchizedek."
In the days of his flesh, Jesus offered up prayers and
supplications, with loud cries and tears, to him who was able
to save him from death, and he was heard because of his
reverence. Although he was a son, he learned obedience
through what he suffered. And being made perfect, he
became the source of eternal salvation to all who obey him,
being designated by God a high priest after the order of
Melchizedek.

About this we have much to say, and it is hard to explain,
since you have become dull of hearing. For though by this
time you ought to be teachers, you need someone to teach
you again the basic principles of the oracles of God. You need
milk, not solid food, for everyone who lives on milk is
unskilled in the word of righteousness, since he is a child. But
solid food is for the mature, for those who have their powers
of discernment trained by constant practice to distinguish
good from evil. ~ Hebrews 5:1–14

Ouch! The author of Hebrews writes that, though his
readers should be able to teach God's Word by now,
they still need to be taught "again the basic principles of
the oracles of God." Some long-time Christians today are
in the same situation. They may have attended church
for years, but they have not studied the Word, so they're
spiritual children. None of us will ever learn or totally
understand everything in God's Word. But are we
growing and learning all the time? Do we know more
than we did last year or even last month? That's why
discipleship is so important; we can't rely on one church

service a week to teach us all we need to know. We need to include other group learning opportunities and private study to become mature Christians. May we never be spiritual babies!

Lord God, it's not always easy to read the Bible and to join with others for classes and studies. But Your Word tells me that if I don't train myself "by constant practice" to distinguish good from evil, I won't mature in the faith. I want to be a mature Christian, Father. Guide me from infancy in the faith to maturity. In the name of Jesus Christ. Amen.

Wednesday in the First Week in Advent

You have said, "I have made a covenant with my chosen one;
   I have sworn to David my servant:
'I will establish your offspring forever,
   and build your throne for all generations.'" ~ Psalm 89:3-4

Centuries before He put His plan into action, God promised to David that His offspring would sit on the throne forever. The people of that day expected a monarchy over their people that would never end, but God had something even more wonderful in mind. He sent His own Son into the world as a tiny baby born in the human line of David to die for our sins to give us eternal life with Him. Jesus, fully man and fully God, human descendant of King David, will rule all the people for eternity. The ones who love and trust in Him will live in glory, love, and peace, and those who reject Him will suffer eternal punishment.

Lord God Almighty, thank You for extending the rule of King David's offspring from just the Jews to everyone, everywhere, always. Every knee will bow and every tongue confess that Jesus Christ is Lord. In His name I pray. Amen.

Thursday in the First Week in Advent

And the Spirit of the Lord shall rest upon him,
   the Spirit of wisdom and understanding,
   the Spirit of counsel and might,
   the Spirit of knowledge and the fear of the Lord.
And his delight shall be in the fear of the Lord.
He shall not judge by what his eyes see,
   or decide disputes by what his ears hear. ~ Isaiah 11:2-3

What a beautiful description of Jesus filled with the Holy Spirit as our ruler and judge! He is wise and understanding, mighty, and knowledgeable. But above all, He delights in the fear of the Lord, and He judges us fairly. We humans tend to judge by what we see and hear. Appearances lead us to believe that the well-dressed man living in a beautiful home is somehow better than the homeless man digging in the dumpster. We hear gossip about a woman and assume she is the immoral person we heard about. But Jesus judges our hearts. He knows us as we really are — not as the image we show to the world or as the words from an unkind person.

Lord God, I am in awe of Jesus Who judges me fairly and loves me beyond measure. This passage reminds me of the wonder of the Godhead — Father, Son, and Holy Spirit. You judge me on my heart, not on externals. So often I fall short and don't live the way Your children should live, the way I want to live. But You know my heart is surrendered to You and judge me accordingly. My heart is filled with gratitude and love for You. In the name of Jesus Christ. Amen.

Friday in the First Week in Advent

Bless the Lord, O my soul!
  O Lord my God, you are very great!
You are clothed with splendor and majesty,
  covering yourself with light as with a garment,
  stretching out the heavens like a tent.
He lays the beams of his chambers on the waters;
he makes the clouds his chariot;
  he rides on the wings of the wind;
he makes his messengers winds,
  his ministers a flaming fire. ~ Psalm 104:1-4

God is clothed in glory, in splendor and majesty beyond our imagination. Such beautiful imagery—riding on the wings of the wind, the clouds his chariot. He deserves our reverence, awe, blessing, and honor. He is our Father. He loves us and wants a personal relationship with us. But sometimes we focus so much on His love and mercy that we overlook His sheer power and might and majesty.

Almighty, all powerful God, I praise You and worship You and give You glory. You alone are the Creator and Sustainer of all things, and Your majesty is beyond my comprehension. Hallelujah! Glory to God! Amen.

Saturday in the First Week in Advent

The Lord God said to the serpent,
"Because you have done this,

cursed are you above all livestock
and above all beasts of the field;
on your belly you shall go,
   and dust you shall eat
   all the days of your life.
I will put enmity between you and the woman,
   and between your offspring and her offspring;
he shall bruise your head,
   and you shall bruise his heel." ~ Genesis 3:14-15

This is the first Messianic prophecy in the Bible. Immediately after the Fall, as soon as man sinned, God offered salvation. The ESV says "he shall bruise your head;" the NIV says "he will crush your head." Jesus will crush, destroy, demolish, obliterate, eradicate that ancient serpent, called the devil, Satan, the deceiver of the whole world. Jesus was promised from the moment the world needed a Savior. He came to earth, died for our sins, and rose to glory. He will come again — we know not when, so we must be ready all the time.

Lord God, Your time is not our time. Your plan has played out over millennia, but it is being carried out on Your schedule, not ours. Yet we know that Your promises are true and will be fulfilled. Just as promised by Old Testament Messianic prophecies, Jesus came to earth to take on our sins and our punishment. And just as promised in the New Testament, Jesus will come again in glory to judge the world. Help me to see past this short life on earth to look forward to eternity in Heaven with You. In the name of Jesus Christ. Amen.

The Second Sunday in Advent

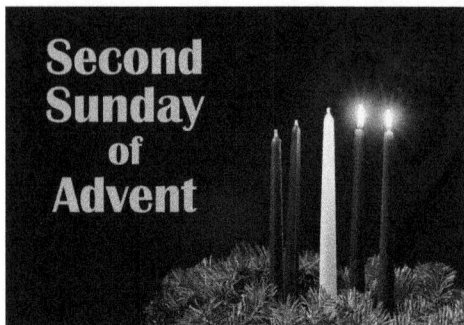

I will tell of the decree:
The Lord said to me, "You are my Son;
today I have begotten you. ~ Psalm 2:7

Muslims — and probably many other people — believe Jesus was a great prophet but not the Son of God. Today's passage tells us that God is the Father, and He has a Son. We now know that Son to be Jesus Christ, the Messiah, our Lord and Savior, the One for whom we wait during Advent.

Father God, it's hard for me to understand the Trinity — how You, the Son, and the Holy Spirit are three persons in one being. But as far back as the Psalms, You were telling us about Jesus — that You had begotten Him. And Jesus told us about the Holy Spirit. You sent the Son to earth before, and I know You will send Him again — this time in glory. I thank You and praise You for sending Jesus to restore my relationship with You by paying for my sins and for the Holy Spirit to guide me. In the name of Jesus Christ, my Lord and Savior. Amen.

Monday in the Second Week in Advent

Therefore the Lord himself will give you a sign. Behold, the virgin shall conceive and bear a son, and shall call his name Immanuel. ~ Isaiah 7:14

Immanuel — "with us is God." Jesus was called Immanuel because He WAS God with us. Although He was fully man, He was also fully God. God Himself — the omnipotent, omniscient, almighty Creator and Sustainer of the universe set aside His majesty and glory and humbled Himself to come to earth as a tiny child, the son of a virgin. We humans don't like to give up any power or acclaim that we might have, but God gave it all up for our sakes. Jesus, though, is now seated at the right hand of the Father in all His glory, and when He returns, He will come in glory.

Almighty and everlasting God, it amazes me that You want to be with me. Jesus came to earth to be with us, and the Holy Spirit lives in the hearts of those who love You — God with us, and God in us. I have known You my entire life, and yet I cannot comprehend how much You love me. Give me a grateful heart, and let me never take You — Father, Son, Holy Spirit — for granted. In the name of Jesus Christ. Amen.

Tuesday in the Second Week in Advent

And the glory of the Lord shall be revealed,
   and all flesh shall see it together,
   for the mouth of the Lord has spoken." ~ Isaiah 40:5

We have never seen the full glory of God, and limitations of our human minds mean we can't even imagine it, either. But one day it will be revealed — on the day Jesus returns. That is the day when every knee shall bow and every tongue confess that Jesus Christ is Lord. But for those who wait until that moment to confess Christ, it will be too late. They will recognize the deity of Christ, but at that time it will not save them. However, those of us who kneel and confess Jesus as our Lord before that great day will be saved. We will not only see His glory at the time of His return, but we will live in it forever. The New Jerusalem is described in Revelation as not needing a sun or moon because God will give it light and Jesus will be its lamp. The glory of the Lord will be on display, and it will be beyond our imaginings.

Lord God, I try to imagine Your glory, but my finite mind cannot grasp the infinite. Although I cannot envision it now, one day I will see You in all Your glory. Thank You that You sent Jesus to save me from my sins so I can dwell in glory with You. In the name of Jesus Christ, my Lord and Savior, who lives and reigns with You and the Holy Ghost forever and ever. Amen.

Wednesday in the Second Week in Advent

But you, O Bethlehem Ephrathah,
  who are too little to be among the clans of Judah,
from you shall come forth for me
  one who is to be ruler in Israel,
whose coming forth is from of old,
  from ancient days. ~ Micah 5:2

This prophecy was written hundreds of years before Jesus's birth, but it foretells the birthplace of the Messiah. It shows that salvation by Jesus was planned long before that, "from ancient days." The Jews must have thought God was moving way too slow, and many think God is moving slow when it comes to Jesus's Second Coming. However, God's timing is perfect; our patience isn't. God always planned for Jesus to be born in a stable in Bethlehem. He always planned to Him to die on the cross and to be raised again from the dead to pay the penalty for our sins and to give us eternal life. And His plans included what most thought too small to be of any importance—Jesus wasn't born in Jerusalem, the city of David, or Rome, the headquarters of the empire, but in a town "too little to be among the clans of Judah." Just as tiny Bethlehem wasn't too insignificant to God, not one of His children—no matter the age, size, status in society, or level of morality—is too insignificant for His redemption. Jesus was born in that crude stable in a little village to save the sinful people in every village, town, city, and country in the world.

Lord God, Your plan astounds me. You knew man would sin before it happened and already had a plan in place to restore the relationship between You and humanity. You told Your people of Your plan thousands of years in advance, and You chose a young girl and a tiny town for the birth of the Savior of the world. Guide me by the Holy Spirit to worship You joyfully, love You fully, and thank You sincerely. In the name of Jesus Christ my Lord. Amen.

Thursday in the Second Week in Advent

For to us a child is born,
   to us a son is given;
and the government shall be upon his shoulder,
   and his name shall be called
Wonderful Counselor, Mighty God,
   Everlasting Father, Prince of Peace.
Of the increase of his government and of peace
   there will be no end,
on the throne of David and over his kingdom,

to establish it and to uphold it
with justice and with righteousness
    from this time forth and forevermore.
The zeal of the Lord of hosts will do this. ~ Isaiah 9:6-7

These magnificent words sung to the stirring music of
Handel's "Messiah" exemplify the Christmas message.
Many of us can't read this passage without the music
echoing in our hearts and minds. Isaiah's words point to
the first coming of Jesus when a child is born, a son is
given. They point to the Second Coming of Christ in
glory and majesty at the end of time, to establish and
uphold His kingdom with justice and righteousness.
And they point to the eternal nature of God's kingdom
under the rulership of Jesus — there will be no end from
this time forth and forevermore. Although the music
was written about 400 years ago, Isaiah prophesied these
words hundreds of years before the birth of Jesus. God's
plan was perfect from the beginning.

*Almighty and everlasting God, thank You for giving us the
holy and majestic words of prophecy and for giving talent to
men to compose stirring and enthralling music. But far above
that, Lord, thank You for fulfilling the prophecy in Jesus's
birth at Christmas and at the end of time in His Second
Coming and eternal rule. As magnificent as these words (and
music of "Messiah") are, Your plan and Jesus's fulfillment of
it are infinitely greater. Make me ever grateful. In the name of
Jesus Christ. Amen.*

Friday in the Second Week in Advent

Oh give thanks to the Lord; call upon his name;
    make known his deeds among the peoples!

Sing to him, sing praises to him;
   tell of all his wondrous works!
Glory in his holy name;
   let the hearts of those who seek the Lord rejoice!
Seek the Lord and his strength;
   seek his presence continually!
Remember the wondrous works that he has done,
   his miracles, and the judgments he uttered,
O offspring of Abraham, his servant,
   children of Jacob, his chosen ones! ~ Psalm 105:1-6

While Advent is a time of preparation and penitence, we should also be remembering all the Lord has done for us. He sent Jesus to be born as a tiny baby – He was born to die for all sins and raised from the dead to give us eternal life. He will come again in glory to take all those who love and serve Him to be with Him for eternity. Yes, He deserves our praise and thanks and worship!

Thank You, Lord God, for all the blessings You give me in this life, but especially for Jesus's giving up His glory to come to earth to die for me, to redeem me and reconcile me to you. I praise You, worship You, and glorify You. In the name of Jesus Christ, my Lord. Amen.

Saturday in the Second Week in Advent

Shout for joy to God, all the earth;
   sing the glory of his name;
   give to him glorious praise!
Say to God, "How awesome are your deeds!
   So great is your power that your enemies come cringing to you.
All the earth worships you

---

and sings praises to you;
    they sing praises to your name." Selah

Come and see what God has done:
    he is awesome in his deeds toward the children of man.
He turned the sea into dry land;
    they passed through the river on foot.
There did we rejoice in him,
    who rules by his might forever,
whose eyes keep watch on the nations—
    let not the rebellious exalt themselves. Selah ~ Psalm 66:1-7

Awesome has become a favored popular expression. I've heard people call coffee *awesome*, declare that it's *awesome* that I'm going to be at an event, and pronounce *awesome* when they like something someone says. The use of the word *awesome* for ordinary, mundane things cheapens it in my mind. Awesome means inspiring awe reverence, admiration, fear. God is awesome; His creation is awesome; His deeds are awesome. How can a cup of coffee or a banal comment be described in the same way as the Holy God, the Creator of all things, the Savior of the world? I will save words like *awesome* and *awe-inspiring* for the One who truly does deserve awe.

Almighty and Holy God, You are awesome, awe-inspiring, majestic, celestial, exalted — beyond words. May I never cheapen Your glory by thinking anything on earth is worthy of the exaltation and worship that rightly belongs only to You. In the name of my Lord and Savior, Jesus Christ. Amen.

The Third Sunday in Advent

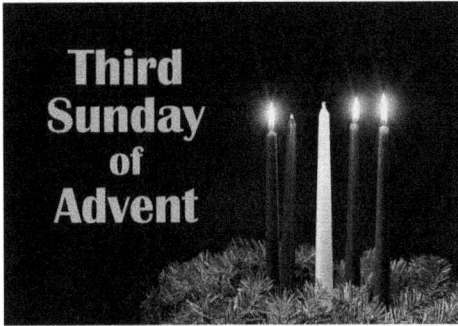

And Jesus said, "I am, and you will see the Son of Man seated at the right hand of Power, and coming with the clouds of heaven." ~ Mark 14:62

Jesus gave this answer in response to the chief priest asking Him if He was the Christ. "I am." Jesus is the Christ, the Lord, the great I AM. He is seated at the right hand of God and will come again in glory. In Advent, we are preparing for this Second Coming as well as for the coming of the babe in the manger. There will be a huge contrast in the coming of the baby and the Second Coming, but the One coming in both is the great I AM.

Lord God Almighty, I am in awe that the great I AM, Jesus, the Second Person of the Trinity, came to earth as a tiny infant and that He will come again in glory at the end of the time. And to think that He was born, suffered, was crucified, was buried, and rose again for me – to cleanse me of my sins is truly awesome. In His Name I pray. Amen.

Monday in the Third Week of Advent

Your throne, O God, is forever and ever.
   The scepter of your kingdom is a scepter of uprightness.
Psalm 45:6

Forever and ever. I read those words, but I can't really comprehend them. Time in this world is finite. We measure the days, weeks, months, and years, and we know that at some point our life here will end. But if we love and trust fully in Jesus, we will be with Him for eternity. Time will never end. No one will get old and die; no babies will be killed in the womb; no one will end his life in an accident. And the ruler of the eternal kingdom will wield a scepter of uprightness. On this earth, no one is good — not one. But in God's eternal kingdom, righteousness will rule.

Eternal, everlasting God, sometimes time seems to move so slowly; other times it seems to move so fast. In this life, time will end. I look forward to an eternity of uprightness under Your rule. In the name of Jesus Christ. Amen.

Tuesday in the Third Week in Advent

"Therefore, thus says the Lord God to them: Behold, I, I myself will judge between the fat sheep and the lean sheep. Because you push with side and shoulder, and thrust at all the weak with your horns, till you have scattered them abroad, I will rescue my flock; they shall no longer be a prey. And I will judge between sheep and sheep. And I will set up over them one shepherd, my servant David, and he shall feed them: he shall feed them and be their shepherd. ~ Ezekiel 34:20-23

People who have power, prestige, wealth, or physical strength sometimes use their strength to push aside weaker, less successful people. But through His prophet, God has promised to rescue His sheep, weak and battered as they may be. He carried through on that promise when He sent His Son to become a man, die on the cross, and rise again. Jesus, the Son of David, will feed us and care for us. All we have to do is love

Him and one another and surrender our wills to His. His plans are always better than ours, even when we don't understand.

Holy God, thank You that You care for Your sheep so much that You sent Your Son to die to cleanse us of our sins and to rise again to give us eternal life. Guide me through the Holy Spirit to do Your will and to follow the Good Shepherd, Jesus Christ, my Lord and Savior. In His name I pray. Amen.

Wednesday in the Third Week in Advent

I will be to him a father, and he shall be to me a son. I will not take my steadfast love from him, as I took it from him who was before you, but I will confirm him in my house and in my kingdom forever, and his throne shall be established forever.
~ 1 Chronicles 17:13-14

God spoke these words to King David through the prophet Nathan a thousand years before Jesus came to earth. Sometimes we think God doesn't hear us because He doesn't seem to answer us as soon as we'd like. But God's timing is not our timing. He promised Jesus thousands of years before He came to earth, and He has promised that Jesus will come again. We can trust that it will happen, but we can't know when. In the meantime, He is sitting on the throne, just as God promised.

Father God, thank You that You always keep Your promises, that You are always working even when I can't see it. Remind me when I doubt and worry about anything that You are in control and that Your plan is perfect. In the name of Jesus Christ, my Lord and Savior. Amen.

Thursday in the Third Week in Advent

The Lord has sworn
  and will not change his mind,
"You are a priest forever
  after the order of Melchizedek." ~ Psalm 110:4

Abraham worshipped and tithed to Melchizedek, who served Abraham bread and wine. Melchizedek was not in the order of Aaron so was not eligible to be a priest under the law. Yet he was known as the King of Salem (thought to be Jerusalem) and priest of the most high God. Likewise, Jesus is both priest and king, and God has promised He will be both forever.

God Most High, I worship and serve Jesus as both priest and king and know He will be both forever. In His name I pray. Amen.

Friday in the Third Week in Advent

"For thus says the Lord God: Behold, I, I myself will search for my sheep and will seek them out. As a shepherd seeks out his flock when he is among his sheep that have been scattered, so will I seek out my sheep, and I will rescue them from all places where they have been scattered on a day of clouds and thick darkness." ~ Ezekiel 34:11-12

We may think we have to search for God, but it's the other way around. He is the One who searches for us. We may think our salvation is dependent on our own actions, but the only thing we have to do is to respond to the Good Shepherd who rescues us. Even if we are in heavy clouds and thick darkness, He will find us.

Thank You, Lord God, that's it not up to me to find You. My responsibility is to respond to You. I love You and believe Jesus is my Lord and Savior. I put my total trust in Him. In His name I pray. Amen.

Saturday in the Third Week in Advent

"Behold, I send my messenger, and he will prepare the way before me. And the Lord whom you seek will suddenly come to his temple; and the messenger of the covenant in whom you delight, behold, he is coming, says the Lord of hosts. But who can endure the day of his coming, and who can stand when he appears? For he is like a refiner's fire and like fullers' soap. He will sit as a refiner and purifier of silver, and he will purify the sons of Levi and refine them like gold and silver, and they will bring offerings in righteousness to the Lord. ~ Malachi 3:1-3

The first time Jesus came to earth, He came as a helpless baby. When He returns, He will come in all His power and majesty and glory, and "who can endure the day...?" If we were judged by our own thoughts, words, and deeds, we would all be consigned to Hell. Praise be to God that we are righteous if we love Jesus because He took our sins upon Himself and gave us His righteousness. When He comes again to judge the world, He will see His righteousness in us.

Thank You, Lord, that You see me as righteous because You see Jesus's righteousness when You look at me. In His name. Amen.

Fourth Sunday in Advent

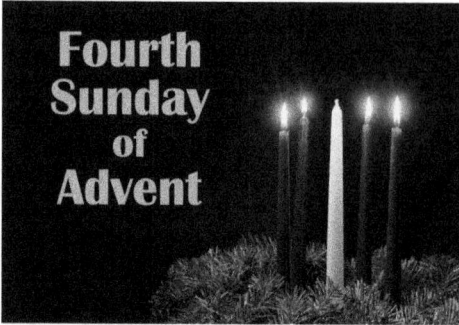

In the sixth month the angel Gabriel was sent from God to a city of Galilee named Nazareth, to a virgin betrothed to a man whose name was Joseph, of the house of David. And the virgin's name was Mary. And he came to her and said, "Greetings, O favored one, the Lord is with you!" But she was greatly troubled at the saying, and tried to discern what sort of greeting this might be. And the angel said to her, "Do not be afraid, Mary, for you have found favor with God. And behold, you will conceive in your womb and bear a son, and you shall call his name Jesus. He will be great and will be called the Son of the Most High. And the Lord God will give to him the throne of his father David, and he will reign over the house of Jacob forever, and of his kingdom there will be no end."

And Mary said to the angel, "How will this be, since I am a virgin?"

And the angel answered her, "The Holy Spirit will come upon you, and the power of the Most High will overshadow you; therefore the child to be born will be called holy—the Son of God. And behold, your relative Elizabeth in her old age has also conceived a son, and this is the sixth month with her who was called barren. For nothing will be impossible with God." And Mary said, "Behold, I am the servant of the Lord; let it be to me according to your word." And the angel departed from her. ~ Luke 1:26-38

I always want to be like Mary, but, alas, I'm more like many other people God has called through the years. Instead of saying, like Mary, "let it be according to your word," I say, like Moses, "Lord, I stutter." Or, like Gideon, "I am the least…" But Mary simply said, "I am the servant of the Lord" and accepted what God asked her to do. May I be more like Mary!

Lord God, give me a willing heart like Mary to respond "let it be …" whenever You ask me to do something – whether it be a general command You have given all Your servants (love your neighbor as yourself) or a specific duty You've assigned me to do for Your Kingdom. In the name of Jesus Christ. Amen.

Monday in the Fourth Week in Advent

How beautiful upon the mountains
   are the feet of him who brings good news,
who publishes peace, who brings good news of happiness,
   who publishes salvation,
     who says to Zion, "Your God reigns." ~ Isaiah 52:7

What better news could we carry than the story of God sending His Son Jesus to be born at Christmas to later die for our sins and rise again to give us eternal life! The good news of peace, happiness, and salvation. The message that our God reigns.

Lord God, let my feet carry me where I need to go to bring the good news of Jesus. Put the words in my mouth and lead me in the way I act so my actions are consistent with Your message. In the name of Jesus Christ. Amen.

Christmas Eve

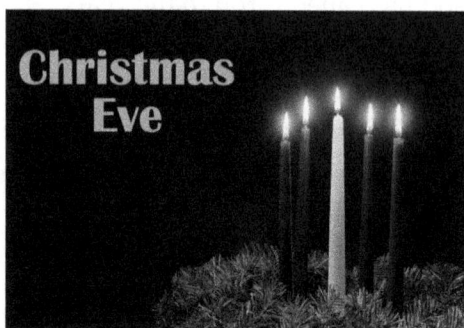

And Mary said,
"My soul magnifies the Lord,
  and my spirit rejoices in God my Savior,
for he has looked on the humble estate of his servant.
  For behold, from now on all generations will call me blessed;
for he who is mighty has done great things for me,
  and holy is his name.
And his mercy is for those who fear him
  from generation to generation.
He has shown strength with his arm;
  he has scattered the proud in the thoughts of their hearts;
he has brought down the mighty from their thrones
  and exalted those of humble estate;
he has filled the hungry with good things,
  and the rich he has sent away empty.
He has helped his servant Israel,
  in remembrance of his mercy,
as he spoke to our fathers,
  to Abraham and to his offspring forever." ~ Luke 1:46-55

The Magnificat is one of the canticles in the Evening Prayer service in the *1928 Book of Common Prayer*. I love when we chant it in Evensong. Mary spoke these words after the angel told her she would give birth to the

Savior. She recognized that the prophecies of the Messiah were being answered through the child she would deliver, and she praised God for fulfilling His promises. She thanked God for her role in His salvation of the world, and she praised Him for His might, mercy, strength, and salvation. She praised Him for His mercy toward the humble and meek and for His judging people, not by wealth or power or pride, but by their fear of the Lord.

Lord God, I want to be among the humble and meek, among those who fear You, among those to whom You show mercy. Mold me into the person You want me to be. In the name of Jesus Christ. Amen.

Christmas Day

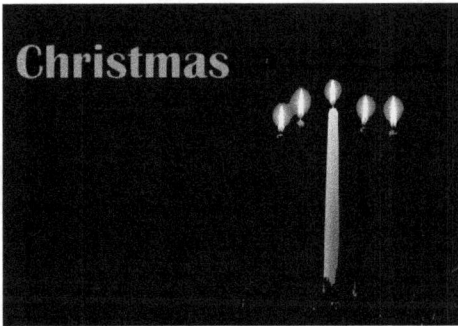

In those days a decree went out from Caesar Augustus that all the world should be registered. This was the first registration when Quirinius was governor of Syria. And all went to be registered, each to his own town. And Joseph also went up from Galilee, from the town of Nazareth, to Judea, to the city of David, which is called Bethlehem, because he was of the house and lineage of David, to be registered with Mary, his betrothed, who was with child. And while they were there, the time came for her to give birth. And she gave birth to her firstborn son and wrapped him in swaddling cloths and laid him in a manger, because there was no place for them in the inn.

And in the same region there were shepherds out in the field, keeping watch over their flock by night. And an angel of the Lord appeared to them, and the glory of the Lord shone around them, and they were filled with great fear. And the angel said to them, "Fear not, for behold, I bring you good news of great joy that will be for all the people. For unto you is born this day in the city of David a Savior, who is Christ the Lord. And this will be a sign for you: you will find a baby wrapped in swaddling cloths and lying in a manger." And suddenly there was with the angel a multitude of the heavenly host praising God and saying,
"Glory to God in the highest,
 and on earth peace among those with whom he is pleased!"
When the angels went away from them into heaven, the shepherds said to one another, "Let us go over to Bethlehem and see this thing that has happened, which the Lord has made known to us." And they went with haste and found Mary and Joseph, and the baby lying in a manger. And when they saw it, they made known the saying that had been told them concerning this child. And all who heard it wondered at what the shepherds told them. But Mary treasured up all these things, pondering them in her heart. And the shepherds returned, glorifying and praising God for all they had heard and seen, as it had been told them.

And at the end of eight days, when he was circumcised, he was called Jesus, the name given by the angel before he was conceived in the womb.

And when the time came for their purification according to the Law of Moses, they brought him up to Jerusalem to present him to the Lord (as it is written in the Law of the Lord, "Every male who first opens the womb shall be called holy to the Lord") and to offer a sacrifice according to what is said in the Law of the Lord, "a pair of turtledoves, or two young pigeons." Now there was a man in Jerusalem, whose name was Simeon, and this man was righteous and devout, waiting for the consolation of Israel, and the Holy Spirit was upon him. And it had been revealed to him by the Holy Spirit that he would not see death before he had seen the Lord's Christ. And he came in the Spirit into the temple, and when the parents brought in the child Jesus, to do for him according to the custom of the Law, he took him up in his arms and blessed God and said,

"Lord, now you are letting your servant depart in peace,
    according to your word;
for my eyes have seen your salvation
    that you have prepared in the presence of all peoples,
a light for revelation to the Gentiles,
    and for glory to your people Israel."

And his father and his mother marveled at what was said about him. And Simeon blessed them and said to Mary his mother, "Behold, this child is appointed for the fall and rising of many in Israel, and for a sign that is opposed (and a sword will pierce through your own soul also), so that thoughts from many hearts may be revealed."

And there was a prophetess, Anna, the daughter of Phanuel, of the tribe of Asher. She was advanced in years, having lived with her husband seven years from when she was a virgin, and then as a widow until she was eighty-four. She did not depart from the temple, worshiping with fasting and prayer night and day. And coming up at that very hour she began to give thanks to God and to speak of him to all who were waiting for the redemption of Jerusalem.

And when they had performed everything according to the Law of the Lord, they returned into Galilee, to their own town of Nazareth. And the child grew and became strong, filled with wisdom. And the favor of God was upon him.
~ Luke 2:1-40

Everything about Jesus's birth was out of the ordinary and miraculous. God had ordained that the Roman decree would declare a tax and require every citizen to return to his hometown—this was in God's plan so Jesus would be born in Bethlehem. A virgin giving birth in the time and place decreed by the Lord, angels singing in the sky, shepherds leaving their flocks to go worship a newborn, an elderly man granted to see the Messiah—all miracles of God. Yet with all these miracles, Mary and Joseph took Jesus to be circumcised and traveled to Jerusalem to present the child in the temple and make a sacrifice. "And when they had performed everything according to the Law of the Lord, they returned into Galilee." Even though Jesus was the Messiah, the Savior of the World, the Second Person of the Trinity, His parents followed the Law and treated Him like any other firstborn son.

Omnipotent and Omniscient Lord, I am constantly amazed at the miracles You perform and at the love You, Jesus, and the Holy Spirit have for Your children. But I'm also in awe of the obedience of Jesus and earthly parents. They followed the Law for His circumcision and presentation, just as they would have if their firstborn had been an ordinary child. What an example! Let me be like Jesus and do Your will. In His name I pray. Amen.

The Second Day of Christmas

He will tend his flock like a shepherd;
    he will gather the lambs in his arms;
he will carry them in his bosom,
    and gently lead those that are with young. ~ Isaiah 40:11

What a comfort to know Jesus is the Good Shepherd! He picks us up when we fall, carries us when we're weak, nourishes us with His own Body and Blood. He protects us from the enemy, and He nurtures us and meets all our needs.

Lord God Almighty, How blessed I am that Jesus is the Good Shepherd, caring for me in good times and bad. Though I am weak, He gives me strength. Though I fall, He lifts me. Though I fail, He covers my sins and errors. Give me a grateful heart. In His name I pray. Amen.

The Third Day of Christmas

"Blessed be the Lord God of Israel,
    for he has visited and redeemed his people
and has raised up a horn of salvation for us
    in the house of his servant David,
as he spoke by the mouth of his holy prophets from of old,
that we should be saved from our enemies
    and from the hand of all who hate us;
to show the mercy promised to our fathers

and to remember his holy covenant,
the oath that he swore to our father Abraham, to grant us
    that we, being delivered from the hand of our enemies,
might serve him without fear,
    in holiness and righteousness before him all our days.
And you, child, will be called the prophet of the Most High;
    for you will go before the Lord to prepare his ways,
to give knowledge of salvation to his people
    in the forgiveness of their sins,
because of the tender mercy of our God,
    whereby the sunrise shall visit us from on high
to give light to those who sit in darkness and in the shadow of
death,
    to guide our feet into the way of peace." ~ Luke 1:68-79

These are the words of Zechariah upon the birth of his son, John the Baptist. When the angel appeared to Zechariah when he was serving as a priest in the temple, Zechariah was doubtful that his wife, who had been barren for many years, would bear a son. Zechariah was made deaf and dumb for his disbelief, and the words in today's passage are the first he spoke after he was healed after the birth of John. He recognized that John was sent to prepare the way for the Messiah, who was the fulfillment of ancient prophecies. God had promised His people that he would send a Savior for His people, and though it took thousands of year, God, as always, fulfilled His promise.

Lord God Almighty, I thank and praise You that You always keep Your promises. Even when it seems to me that nothing is happening, remind me that Your timing is not my timing — but Your timing is perfect. You are never late, but always on time. Give me patience and faith as I wait. In the name of Jesus Christ, my Lord and Savior. Amen.

The Fourth Day of Christmas (Holy Innocents)

Now after Jesus was born in Bethlehem of Judea in the days of Herod the king, behold, wise men from the east came to Jerusalem, saying, "Where is he who has been born king of the Jews? For we saw his star when it rose and have come to worship him." When Herod the king heard this, he was troubled, and all Jerusalem with him; and assembling all the chief priests and scribes of the people, he inquired of them where the Christ was to be born. They told him, "In Bethlehem of Judea, for so it is written by the prophet:

"'And you, O Bethlehem, in the land of Judah,
    are by no means least among the rulers of Judah;
for from you shall come a ruler
    who will shepherd my people Israel.'"

Then Herod summoned the wise men secretly and ascertained from them what time the star had appeared. And he sent them to Bethlehem, saying, "Go and search diligently for the child, and when you have found him, bring me word, that I too may come and worship him." After listening to the king, they went on their way. And behold, the star that they had seen when it rose went before them until it came to rest over the place where the child was. When they saw the star, they rejoiced exceedingly with great joy. And going into the house, they saw the child with Mary his mother, and they fell down and worshiped him. Then, opening their treasures, they offered him gifts, gold and frankincense and myrrh. And being warned in a dream not to return to Herod, they departed to their own country by another way.

Now when they had departed, behold, an angel of the Lord appeared to Joseph in a dream and said, "Rise, take the child and his mother, and flee to Egypt, and remain there until I tell you, for Herod is about to search for the child, to destroy him." And he rose and took the child and his mother by night and departed to Egypt and remained there until the death of Herod. This was to fulfill what the Lord had spoken by the prophet, "Out of Egypt I called my son."

Then Herod, when he saw that he had been tricked by the wise men, became furious, and he sent and killed all the male children in Bethlehem and in all that region who were two years old or under, according to the time that he had ascertained from the wise men. Then was fulfilled what was spoken by the prophet Jeremiah:

"A voice was heard in Ramah,
    weeping and loud lamentation,
Rachel weeping for her children;
    she refused to be comforted, because they are no more."

But when Herod died, behold, an angel of the Lord appeared in a dream to Joseph in Egypt, saying, "Rise, take the child and his mother and go to the land of Israel, for those who sought the child's life are dead." And he rose and took the child and his mother and went to the land of Israel. But when he heard that Archelaus was reigning over Judea in place of his father Herod, he was afraid to go there, and being warned in a dream he withdrew to the district of Galilee. And he went and lived in a city called Nazareth, so that what was spoken by the prophets might be fulfilled, that he would be called a Nazarene. ~ Matthew 2:1–23

Right after Christmas, as part of the story of the birth of Jesus, Herod murders babies. He was so enraged that the Wise Men didn't lead him directly to the promised King that he was determined to kill every baby who could possibly be that child. Of course, God had protected Jesus and warned Joseph to escape with Jesus and Mary, but my heart bleeds for the babies who were killed and for their families. In a small community, many of the families with young children were probably related, so one extended family may have lost several infants. Those little ones were martyrs "in deed but not in will." Unlike the martyrs who knowingly and willingly died for their faith (martyrs in will and deed) or disciples who were willing to die for their faith but weren't killed (martyrs in will but not deed), these babies and their families had no choice. Yet they sacrificed their lives and their families sacrificed their children to further God's plan for Jesus as the Savior of the world.

Lord God of mercy, this tragic and evil event shortly after Jesus's birth demonstrates how much the world needed and still needs a Savior. One man was so selfish and power-hungry that he murdered babies to protect his sovereignty. Today mothers and their accomplices kill babies in the womb to protect their selfish desires. We still need Jesus, Lord. Open the eyes and hearts of all who do not know Him and draw them to Him. In His name I pray. Amen.

The Fifth Day of Christmas

Then I saw a new heaven and a new earth, for the first heaven and the first earth had passed away, and the sea was no more. And I saw the holy city, new Jerusalem, coming down out of heaven from God, prepared as a bride adorned for her husband. And I heard a loud voice from the throne saying, "Behold, the dwelling place of God is with man. He will dwell with them, and they will be his people, and God himself will be with them as their God. He will wipe away every tear from their eyes, and death shall be no more, neither shall there be mourning, nor crying, nor pain anymore, for the former things have passed away."

And he who was seated on the throne said, "Behold, I am making all things new." Also he said, "Write this down, for these words are trustworthy and true." And he said to me, "It is done! I am the Alpha and the Omega, the beginning and the end. To the thirsty I will give from the spring of the water of life without payment. The one who conquers will have this heritage, and I will be his God and he will be my son. ~ Revelation 21:1-7

Hallelujah! Jesus came into the world as a baby at Christmas to become the man who would die for our sins and rise again to give us eternal life. This passage describes what our world will be like after Jesus returns. What glory we have to look forward to.

Merciful and loving God, I look forward to the day when there be no more mourning, no more crying, no more pain. Thank You that You sent Jesus to become sin for us so that we would be forgiven of our sins and made new to live with You in the new Jerusalem. In His name. Amen.

The Sixth Day of Christmas

Behold, I stand at the door and knock. If anyone hears my voice and opens the door, I will come in to him and eat with him, and he with me. The one who conquers, I will grant him to sit with me on my throne, as I also conquered and sat down with my Father on his throne. He who has an ear, let him hear what the Spirit says to the churches.'" ~ Revelation 3:20-22

Jesus is knocking on the door of our hearts asking us to let Him in. If we answer, we will sit with Him on His throne in Heaven! Why would we hesitate to open the door? Too often, we have a short-term, earthly perspective. If we had an eternal perspective, we would hurry to let Jesus in and look forward to sitting on the throne with Him.

Heavenly Father, my heart is open to Jesus. I invite Him in and give praise and thanks for the salvation that He brings. In His name I pray. Amen.

The Seventh Day of Christmas

And God spoke to Israel in visions of the night and said, "Jacob, Jacob." And he said, "Here I am." Then he said, "I am God, the God of your father. Do not be afraid to go down to Egypt, for there I will make you into a great nation. I myself will go down with you to Egypt, and I will also bring you up again, and Joseph's hand shall close your eyes."

Then Jacob set out from Beersheba. The sons of Israel carried Jacob their father, their little ones, and their wives, in the wagons that Pharaoh had sent to carry him. ~ Genesis 46:2-5

God's ways and thoughts are certainly above ours. The Israelites' time in Egypt, including the years of slavery, were all part of God's plan leading to redemption to His Son born at Christmas. I can't understand this plan with my finite, human mind. But I know that it is good because God is good. And I see the end and am so glad that Jesus died for my sins and gave me eternal life. Did God send Jacob and his family into Egypt just to show His power and might hundreds of years later when He miraculously brought them out of slavery? I don't know how or why God has done what He has, but I am grateful beyond words that all He did led to salvation for me and anyone who believes.

Eternal, almighty God, Your plan is beyond my comprehension, but I do understand that it will all turn out the way it's supposed to. I look forward to the new heaven and the new earth when all Your people will live with You in the new Jerusalem, where there is no pain, no tears, no sorrow. Thank You for including me in Your plan and Your love. In the name of Jesus Christ. Amen.

The Eighth Day of Christmas (The Circumcision of Christ)

And a vision appeared to Paul in the night: a man of Macedonia was standing there, urging him and saying, "Come over to Macedonia and help us." And when Paul had seen the vision, immediately we sought to go on into Macedonia, concluding that God had called us to preach the gospel to them. ~ Acts 16:9-10

The Bible is filled with stories of dreams and visions sent from God to lead His people. There's nothing in the Bible that says He no longer uses dreams and visions to send messages to His people. We know that dreams and visions of Jesus often open the eyes of Muslims and lead them to Christ. Maybe in our sophistication and education, we don't notice the supernatural messages from the Lord. Maybe He still speaks to us if we only pay attention. I know I have had several dreams that called me to action and a vision of my late husband shortly after his death that gave me great peace. How often, though, have I missed what God is telling me because I don't recognize a dream or a vision? Paul didn't hesitate when he had the dream; immediately, he started making plans to do what God called him to do. He didn't question or procrastinate, as I sometimes do.

Thank You, Lord God, for the dreams and vision I have been blessed to receive from You. Open the eyes of my heart and mind so that I never miss a message You are sending me in whatever form it takes. I want to be like Paul. When I have a dream or vision or persistent thought that I believe comes from You, give me the discernment to recognize Your call and the courage and faith to do it. In the name of Jesus Christ. Amen.

The Ninth Day of Christmas

Make a joyful noise to the Lord, all the earth!
  Serve the Lord with gladness!
  Come into his presence with singing!

Know that the Lord, he is God!
  It is he who made us, and we are his;
  we are his people, and the sheep of his pasture.

Enter his gates with thanksgiving,
  and his courts with praise!
  Give thanks to him; bless his name!

For the Lord is good;
  his steadfast love endures forever,
  and his faithfulness to all generations. ~ Psalm 100

God is good all the time. All the time God is good. Even when we can't see His goodness. Even when things go wrong. Even when we don't understand. He is still good. He still deserves our praise for His goodness and faithfulness.

Lord, help me always to remember Your goodness, to know that Your plan is perfect even when I don't understand. Let me praise You forever, no matter my circumstances. In the name of Jesus Christ. Amen.

The Tenth Day of Christmas

And she vowed a vow and said, "O Lord of hosts, if you will indeed look on the affliction of your servant and remember me and not forget your servant, but will give to your servant a son, then I will give him to the Lord all the days of his life, and no razor shall touch his head." ...

But Hannah did not go up, for she said to her husband, "As soon as the child is weaned, I will bring him, so that he may appear in the presence of the Lord and dwell there forever." ~ 1 Samuel 1:11, 22

Hannah was desperate for a son. In that time and place, a woman who was barren was disgraced. She was so desperate for a child that she promised God that if He would only give her a son, she would give him to the service of the Lord. God answered her prayer, and Hannah kept her promise. After he was weaned, she took the child to the temple to serve the Lord. That child who was an answer to prayer was Samuel, a great prophet of Israel. God answered Hannah's prayer, and she kept her promise. Hannah's stigma was removed and she enjoyed a short time with her baby, but then she gave him up. She was content just to be a mother, even if she couldn't do all that mothers do.

Eternal, holy God, please make me more like Hannah. When she was in distress, she went directly to You in prayer. Forgive me when I complain and moan to others rather than taking my problems to You first and only. Hannah was satisfied with bearing a son and giving him up to You. So often I want more instead of being satisfied with the many blessings I have. Forgive me, Lord, and give me a grateful heart. In the name of Jesus Christ. Amen.

The Eleventh Day of Christmas

I appeal to you therefore, brothers, by the mercies of God, to present your bodies as a living sacrifice, holy and acceptable to God, which is your spiritual worship. Do not be conformed to this world, but be transformed by the renewal of your mind, that by testing you may discern what is the will of God, what is good and acceptable and perfect. ~ Romans 12:1-2

It's so easy for us to be conformed to this world. It's happened to so many Christians on a grand scale, and it happens to all of us to some degree. How many Christians are divorced or believe in "a woman's right to choose" (a euphemism for killing a baby) or accept homosexual "marriage" or live with their sexual partners before marriage or think it's okay to take office supplies home from work and take long breaks and lunch periods while on the clock? Or all of the above? All of us sin and fall short of the glory of God, but if we love the Lord and claim to be His disciples, we will study His Word and pray for His guidance. We will aim for what is good and acceptable and perfect.

Lord God, please forgive me when I live like the world around me rather than being transformed and discerning Your will. Lead me in Your ways and turn me from the ways of the world. In the name of Jesus Christ, my Lord and Savior. Amen.

The Twelfth Day of Christmas (Eve of the Epiphany)

He who has prepared us for this very thing is God, who has given us the Spirit as a guarantee.

So we are always of good courage. We know that while we are at home in the body we are away from the Lord, for we walk by faith, not by sight. Yes, we are of good courage, and we would rather be away from the body and at home with the Lord. ~ 2 Corinthians 5:5-8

Sometimes, I get anxious when I can't see what's ahead. I worry about the future and fear what might happen. But God's word tells us to "walk by faith, not by sight." God doesn't always let us see what's ahead, but He always has a perfect plan, and He's always there with us. When the road gets rough and we can't see around the next bend, God carries us over the rough spots. He always knows what is around the bend, and He is always in control. We don't always understand, but we know that He is good and His plan is perfect.

Holy Father, forgive me when I doubt and fear because I can't see the road ahead of me. Help me to remember that You know the road and the Holy Spirit is traveling it with me. Give me the comfort of remembering that You are always in control, and no matter what else the future holds, it always holds You. In the name of Jesus Christ, my Lord and Savior. Amen.

The Epiphany of Our Lord

Now after Jesus was born in Bethlehem of Judea in the days of Herod the king, behold, wise men from the east came to Jerusalem, saying, "Where is he who has been born king of the Jews? For we saw his star when it rose and have come to worship him." ...

And behold, the star that they had seen when it rose went before them until it came to rest over the place where the child was. When they saw the star, they rejoiced exceedingly with great joy. And going into the house, they saw the child with Mary his mother, and they fell down and worshiped him. Then, opening their treasures, they offered him gifts, gold and frankincense and myrrh. And being warned in a dream not to return to Herod, they departed to their own country by another way. ~ Matthew 2:1-2, 9-12

The word *Epiphany* means showing or manifestation. On Epiphany, Jesus was shown to the Gentiles when the Three Kings visited and worshipped Him. The wise men were foreigners, not Jews; they were probably pagan priests or astrologers. Yet the star led them to the king of the Jews to worship and bring gifts, revealing that the Messiah and God's promises were not for the Jews only, but also for the Gentiles. The gifts the Magi brought were gifts traditionally given to royalty, manifesting that the tiny baby was a king.

Lord God Almighty, how blessed I and all Gentiles are that You included us in Your plan of redemption. Your mercies are not for only certain people but are available to anyone who will accept them. Thank You, Lord. In the name of Jesus Christ, my Lord and Savior. Amen.

ARISE, SHINE; FOR YOUR LIGHT HAS COME, AND THE GLORY OF THE LORD HAS RISEN UPON YOU.

ISAIAH 60:1, NRSV

Finding God in the Everyday
by Lillie Ammann, author of *The Glory of the Lord*

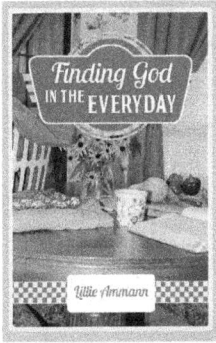

We expect to find God in church and in our private devotions. But have you ever wondered where He is the rest of the time—especially when things go wrong? With humor and poignancy, author Lillie Ammann shares in these ninety devotionals how she finds God in the everyday experiences of her life.

Finding God in the Everyday is available in paperback and ebook formats through online stores or directly from the author.

If you like the smell of cookies in the oven and watching reruns of The Waltons, you will love the folksy flavor of Finding God in the Everyday. ~ Molly Noble Bull, Christian romance author

Lillie has written a refreshingly insightful book. This book is practical, inspiring, and highly readable. ~ Terry L. Sumerlin, Conference speaker and author, www.terrysumerlin.com

Lillie Ammann shares stories from her life, showing great insight in how God has used these experiences to help her and others grow in their faith. This book will encourage everyone who reads it to look for God's hand in their daily lives. ~ Janet Kaderli, Christian author

Lillie's ability to view life from a faith perspective encourages her readers to do the same. Stories from her life and Scriptural passages inspire us to rely on God in all circumstances. ~ Jan Kilby, Ph.D., Writing consultant and freelance writer, San Antonio, Texas

www.ingramcontent.com/pod-product-compliance
Lightning Source LLC
Chambersburg PA
CBHW071747020426
42331CB00008B/2217